The Wild Side of Pet
Lizards

Jo Waters

D0230788

www.raintreepublishers.co.uk

Visit our website to find out more information about Raint...

To order:
☎ Phone 44 (0) 1865 888112
📄 Send a fax to 44 (0) 1865 314091
💻 Visit the Raintree Bookshop at **www.raintreepublishers.co.uk**

First published in Great Britain by Raintree, Halley Court, Jordan Hill, Oxford OX2 8EJ, part of Harcourt Education.
Raintree is a registered trademark of Harcourt Education Ltd.

Editorial: Melanie Copland and Saskia Besier
Design: Richard Parker and
Tinstar Design Ltd (www.tinstar.co.uk)
Picture Research: Maria Joannou and Alison Prior
Production: Jonathan Smith

Originated by Ambassador Litho Ltd
Printed and bound in China by South China Printing Company

The paper used to print this book comes from sustainable resources.

ISBN 1 844 43482 6 (hardback)
08 07 06 05 04
10 9 8 7 6 5 4 3 2 1

ISBN 1 844 43489 3 (paperback)
09 08 07 06 05
10 9 8 7 6 5 4 3 2 1

British Library Cataloguing in Publication Data
Waters, Jo
The Wild Side of Pet Lizards
639.3'95
A full catalogue record for this book is available from the British Library.

Acknowledgements
The publishers would like to thank the following for permission to reproduce photographs: Bruce Coleman Collection pp. **5 top** (Alain Compost), **5 bot** (Joe McDonald), **13** (J Watt); Corbis p. **22**, Getty Images pp. **7**, **10** (Photodisc), **17** (Darlyne A. Dr Murawski), **20** (P Lilja); Minden Pictures p. **24**; Nature Picture Library p. **15** (D Kjaer)); NHPA pp. **6** (Stephen Dalton), **12** (D Heuclin), **14** (M Harvey), **16** (B Coster); Oxford Scientific Films pp. **26** (B Kenney), **27** (Densey Clyne Productions), **28** (Animals Animals); Photodisc pp. **4**, **29**; Tudor Photography/Harcourt Education Ltd pp. **9**, **11**, **19**, **21**, **23**, **25**.

Cover photograph of a bearded dragon, reproduced with permission of Tudor Photography/Harcourt Education Ltd. Inset cover photograph of Mediterranean chameleon reproduced with permission of NHPA (John & Sue Buckingham).

The publishers would like to thank Michaela Miller for her assistance in the preparation of this book.

Every effort has been made to contact copyright holders of any material reproduced in this book. Any omissions will be rectified in subsequent printings if notice is given to the publishers.

Contents

Any words appearing in bold, **like this**, are explained in the Glossary.

Was your pet once wild?

You may think that you just have a pet lizard, but really you have a wild animal living in your house. Finding out more about how your pet lives in the wild will help you give it a better life.

Lizards are **reptiles**. They are all **cold-blooded**. This means that their bodies are at the same temperature as their surroundings. They use the sun or the shade to warm up or cool down.

Iguanas are mostly found in North and South America.

4

Wild lizards are the same as the lizards we keep as pets. They are not like other pets. Lizards need special conditions and care to keep them healthy.

Make sure you find out as much as you can before you decide if a lizard is a suitable pet for you.

Have you got room?
Some lizards can grow to over a metre in their first year. As they get older, growth slows but never completely stops!

The Komodo Dragon is the world's largest lizard. It can grow to over 3 metres long and weigh up to 135 kilograms.

Types of lizard

There are over 4700 different **species** of lizard.
These include tiny lizards that are insect-eaters,
and really big meat-eaters.

The main species of lizard are iguanas, chameleons,
geckos, gila monsters, monitors and skinks.
Monitor lizards were probably one of the first
species of lizard alive on the Earth.

Lizard relatives

*Lizards are related to
snakes. They are all
reptiles. All reptiles are
cold-blooded, have scaly
skin and forked tongues.
Alligators, crocodiles,
salamanders and turtles
are also reptiles.*

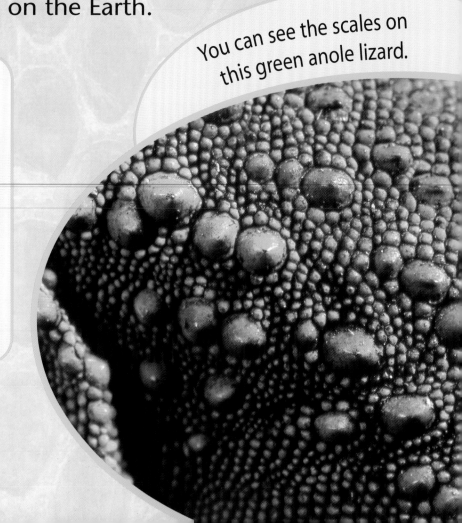

You can see the scales on
this green anole lizard.

Difficult pets

There are lots of types of pet lizard. Many lizards that people buy as pets die very quickly. This is because their owners do not realise how difficult lizards are to look after.

You need to think really hard about whether a lizard is the right pet for you. Lizards such as green iguanas need special care. Monitors grow far too big to make a suitable pet. Chameleons are very fragile and can be hurt by handling.

Some lizards grow extremely large and should only be kept in zoos or special reptile homes.

Where are lizards from?

Most of the world's lizards are found where there is plenty of sun and heat to keep them warm. Some like **humid** air and others prefer to live where it is dry.

North America is home to lizards such as anoles, geckos, collared lizards, iguanas and the gila monster. Africa has large monitor lizards and many types of geckos. Australia has geckos, skinks and many types of monitor lizard, including goannas.

Arctic Circle

North America

Europe

Asia

Africa

Equator

South America

Australia

many lizards
few lizards
no lizards

Antarctic Circle

Antarctica

This map shows where lizards live in the world.

Local reptile clubs or societies are good places to start looking for a pet lizard. They can give support and advice once you have your pet. You can also ask a vet for advice.

A lizard should be alert and have plenty of energy. It should be clean with clear eyes and nose and healthy looking skin.

Captured in the wild

You should never buy lizards that have been taken from the wild. They may have illnesses or diseases. Many lizards that are caught in the wild do not survive the journey to where they are sold.

Lizard habitats

In the wild, lizards are found in different sorts of **habitats**. They can live in deserts, in rainforests and jungles or in rocky places.

Lizards have **adapted** to live in different places. Most lizards need to bask in the sun. The sunlight allows them to absorb **vitamin** D to build healthy skin and bones.

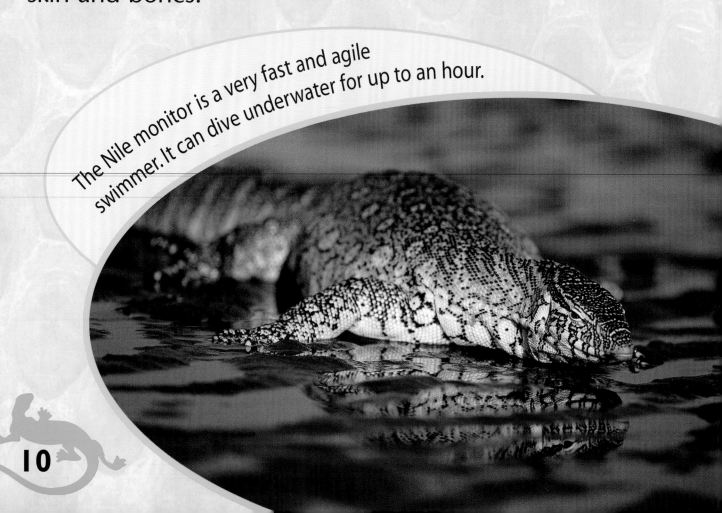

The Nile monitor is a very fast and agile swimmer. It can dive underwater for up to an hour.

Ask an expert what to put in your lizard's vivarium. A desert lizard needs a sand floor, but a rainforest lizard needs leaves and branches.

Lizard homes

Instead of roaming wild, pet lizards usually have to live in a **vivarium**. Vivariums should be made of glass or metal and should not have any sharp edges or wire mesh where lizards might hurt themselves.

Lizards need plenty of air. Stale air can make them ill. Lizards also need heat, but they should always have a place to go to cool down. If your lizard gets too hot, it can die.

Lizard anatomy

Lizards have small heads, short necks and long bodies and tails. Most lizards have teeth on both jaws. Some even have teeth on the roof of their mouths.

Colour change

Some lizards change colour depending on how they are feeling. The green anole is green when warm and relaxed. It goes darker brown when cold or frightened.

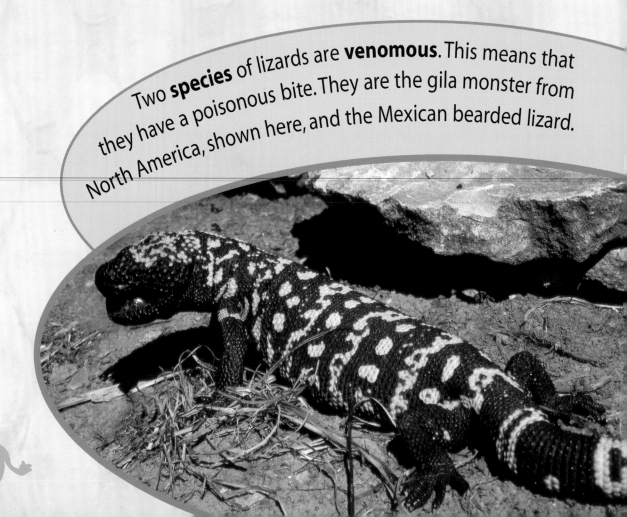

Two **species** of lizards are **venomous**. This means that they have a poisonous bite. They are the gila monster from North America, shown here, and the Mexican bearded lizard.

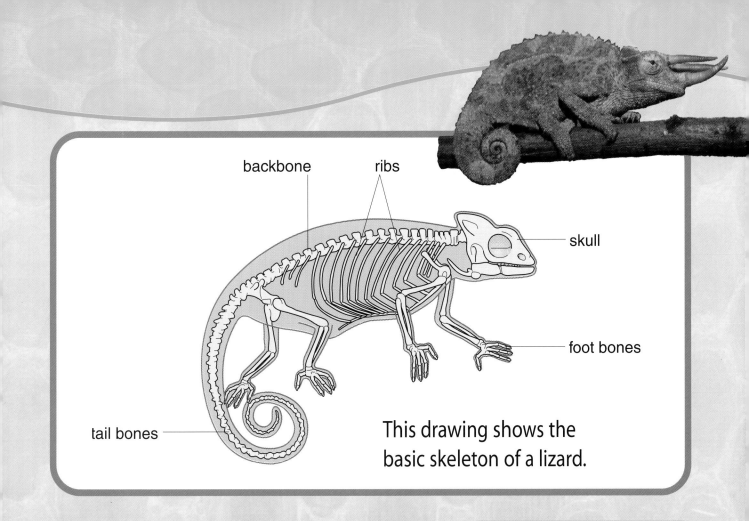

backbone

ribs

skull

foot bones

tail bones

This drawing shows the basic skeleton of a lizard.

Pet lizards have the same **anatomy**, or body parts, as wild lizards. Your pet lizard has scales, short legs with claws, a tail and sharp teeth.

Shedding

*Most lizards **shed** their skins. The outer, dead layer falls off leaving a new skin underneath. Most need **humid**, warm air to shed properly.*

Lizards can have patterned scales, like the gila monster. They may be brightly coloured like the collared lizard or the sawback agamid. They may have spines like the spiny iguana or bearded dragon.

Senses

A lizard's eyes are usually wide apart and set on either side of its head. It needs all-round vision to watch for dangers. Many lizards, such as chameleons and iguanas, can see in colour. In the wild, lizards use skin colour to attract a mate or scare away **predators**.

The Tasmanian blotched blue-tongue lizard has an extraordinary tongue!

Smelling

A lizard uses its tongue to help it smell things. It flicks its tongue out and **particles** stick to it. Special **cells** on the roof of the lizard's mouth smell the particles. Lizards use their sense of smell to find food and warn of enemies.

Your pet lizard may not seem to use its sense of hearing. Lizards have **eardrums** just under the surface of the skin on the sides of their heads. They cannot hear very well.

Special eyes

Some lizards have eyelids and can blink. Others, like geckos, cannot blink. They have clear protective skins over their eyes. They keep their eyes wet by licking them with their tongues.

Some lizards, like chameleons, can use their eyes separately. They can look with one eye in a different direction from the other.

Movement

Some lizards, like chameleons use their tails to grasp things and to balance.

Lizards can only move quickly when they are warm enough. If they are cold they will be sluggish and slow.

Most lizards are very good climbers. They use their flexible toes and sharp claws to cling on.

Some lizards have no legs. They move by using muscles on their bellies. They use their scales to grip the ground.

Flying lizards

The flying dragon lizard lives in South-East Asia and India. It has skin between its legs, which it can spread and use like wings to glide to safety.

Although they cannot run and hunt like wild lizards, pet lizards still need space to move around and exercise in. Lizards need to move to keep their muscles and bones healthy.

Swimming!

Some **reptiles**, such as green iguanas, are good swimmers. They need a small pool, like a paddling pool, to swim in. A big, swimming lizard is not the right pet for you if you have not got much space.

Geckos can climb straight up walls and even on the ceiling. They can do this because they have special gripping pads on their toes.

What do lizards eat?

Most wild lizards are **carnivores** or **insectivores**. Some are **omnivores**, which means they eat meat and plants. Others are **herbivores** and eat only plants. Some lizards only need to eat every 4 to 5 days.

Monitors and tegus are carnivores. Nile monitors eat fish, crabs, eggs, small animals and insects.

Green iguanas and chuckwallas are herbivores. Chuckwallas eat mostly leaves and grasses, with some fruit and flowers. Green iguanas eat mainly leaves.

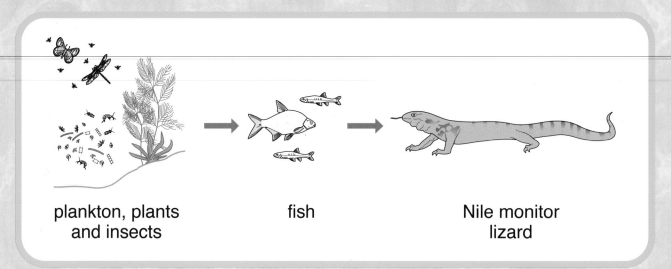

| plankton, plants and insects | fish | Nile monitor lizard |

This is how the Nile monitor fits into a **food chain**.

Lizards may need live food as well as plants and grains.

Carnivorous pet lizards eat dead baby mice, called pinkies, and live insects like crickets and locusts.

Herbivorous pet lizards eat leafy green vegetables like dandelion leaves and flowers. They can also eat grains like wheat, oats and rice.

Vitamins

*It is difficult to feed pet lizards what they eat in the wild. It is important to help them with extra **vitamins**.*

Your lizard should have a clean, full bowl of water at all times. Otherwise it will get ill.

Hunting and handling

Some lizards hunt food such as small animals and insects. They find their **prey** by lying in wait and watching for movement. Other lizards search out tasty plants to eat. They find their food by smell.

Tongues

Chameleons have amazing tongues. They are sticky and can make a cup shape on the end. A chameleon uses its tongue to catch insects. It shoots its tongue out, swipes the insect and pulls it into its mouth, all in a split second.

This insect was too slow!

Most lizards have very strong jaws for hunting. A bite from a big lizard like an iguana can really hurt and draw blood. They are not really suitable pets and should only be kept by experts.

Lizards do not enjoy human contact. If you want a pet to cuddle, lizards are not for you.

Watch that tail!

Some lizards, like curly-tails, can 'drop' their tails. This is to escape being caught. They can lose their tails if you grab them suddenly or in the wrong way, so be careful.

Do lizards live in groups?

In the wild, most lizards live alone. Males can fight if they meet.

Body language

Most lizards **communicate** by using body language. Aggressive lizards will open their mouths when they are frightened or angry. Others may puff up or lash their tails.

Many lizards have 'beards' or frills around their head and neck area. They can extend these when they want to show-off or to threaten another lizard.

The frilled lizard from Australia and New Guinea has a large frill around its neck. It uses this to frighten its enemies.

Dab lizards will usually live happily together.

You can keep some lizards together, even though they would live alone in the wild. Ask an expert before you put lizards together. Males should be separated as soon as they are adult. Otherwise they will fight.

Always check that groups of lizards are not fighting. Bites and scratches can make a lizard very ill.

Unfriendly animals

Lizards are not very friendly animals. They may sometimes come hurrying over to greet you, but only if they think food is coming.

Sleeping

All lizards need sleep. Most lizards are active during the day. This is because their bodies need warmth from the sun to work properly. There are some unusual lizards like geckos, which are active at night.

Lizards usually sleep in gaps in rocks, burrows or holes in trees and logs.

Green anoles sleep on the tips of leaves. If a **predator** attacks them, the anoles will feel the movement, wake up and escape.

Hibernation

Most lizards **hibernate** through winter. Hibernation is a very deep sleep. The lizard's body goes into slow-motion and uses very little energy.

In the wild, lizards wake up to hunt and keep warm. Well-kept pet lizards do not need to, because they will be fed and kept warm. They rest or sleep most of the time.

Keeping an eye out

Some lizards can sleep with one eye open. Half of their brain is asleep and half of it is working, keeping an eye out for danger. They only do this if they feel scared.

Make sure your lizard has somewhere to hide and sleep. It needs a safe place just as it would in the wild.

Life cycle of lizards

Some lizards only live for a short time, while others can live for many years. Bearded dragons live for about 10 years. The Mona ground iguana can live for over 30 years.

Are lizards good parents?

*Many lizards, like Komodo dragons, lay their eggs and then leave them to hatch on their own. The eggs are buried, but **predators** and even other Komodo dragons often find them and eat them.*

Many lizards lay eggs. Other lizards, like skinks, give birth to live babies.

These are baby collared lizards.

Pet lizards may not live as long as wild lizards. This is because it is very hard to give pet lizards the healthy life they would have in the wild.

Baby lizards

Lizards do not often have babies when kept as pets. But there are some, such as geckos, anoles and collared lizards, which can.

Common problems

Humans often harm lizards. Wild lizards are caught to sell as pets. Many lizards die before they are sold. Lizard **habitats**, such as rainforests, deserts and rivers, can be **polluted** or destroyed by industry and farming.

Wild lizards can also suffer from diseases. Most lizards are hunted by **predators** as well. Their predators include other lizards, birds of **prey**, such as eagles, and wild cats.

The San Diego coast horned lizard is endangered.

In danger!
*The following **species** of lizard are **endangered**:*
- *Jamaican iguana*
- *Anegada island iguana*
- *Komodo dragon*
- *San Diego coast horned lizard.*

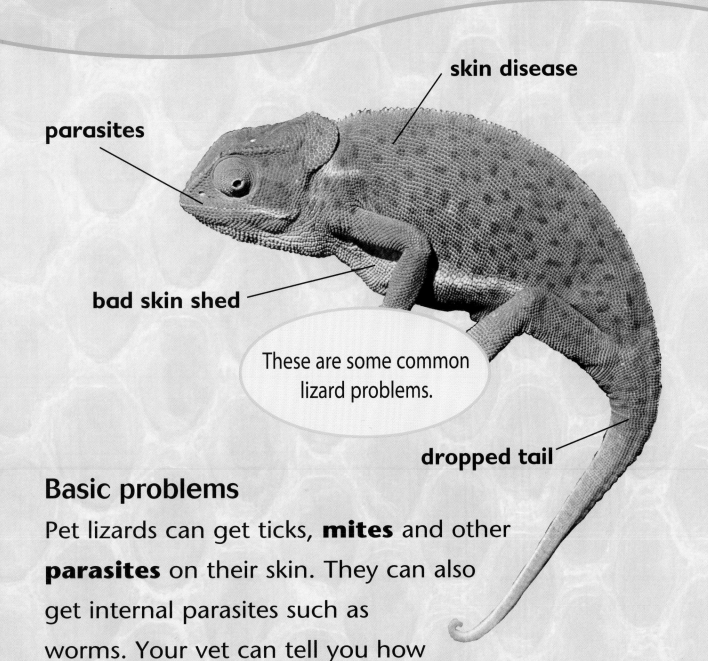

skin disease

parasites

bad skin shed

These are some common lizard problems.

dropped tail

Basic problems

Pet lizards can get ticks, **mites** and other
parasites on their skin. They can also
get internal parasites such as
worms. Your vet can tell you how
to treat different parasites.

If your lizard does not get enough sunlight or
ultraviolet light, it can get very dull and lifeless.
It may also get **brittle** bones and eventually die.

Find out for yourself

A good owner will always want to learn more about keeping a pet lizard. To find out more information about lizards, you can look in other books and on the Internet.

Books to read

Keeping Lizards (Unusual Pets), David Manning
(Barron's Educational Series, 2000)
Keeping Unusual Pets: Geckos, Sonia Hernandez-Divers
(Heinemann Library, 2002)

Using the Internet

Explore the Internet to find out about lizards. Websites can change, so if one of the links below no longer works, don't worry. Use a search engine, such as *www.yahooligans.com* or *www.internet4kids.com*. You could try searching using the keywords 'lizard', 'pet' and 'geckos'.

Websites

A good basic site for lizard care can be found at:
www.vetulike.co.uk/advice/exotic%20pets/lizardsgencare.htm

The British Herpetological Society has a website full of lizard information: *www.thebhs.org*

Disclaimer
All the Internet addresses (URLs) given in this book were valid at the time of going to press. However, due to the dynamic nature of the Internet, some addresses may have changed, or sites may have ceased to exist since publication. While the author and publishers regret any inconvenience this may cause readers, no responsibility for any such changes can be accepted by either the author or the publishers.

Glossary

adapted become used to living in certain conditions

anatomy how the body is made

brittle not strong and can break very easily

carnivore animal that only eats meat

cell smallest part that makes up a living thing

cold-blooded when blood is the same temperature as the air around it

communicate to make yourself understood

eardrum a thin layer of skin which allows animals to hear

endangered in danger of dying out or being killed

food chain links between different animals that feed on each other and on plants

habitat where an animal or plant lives

herbivore animal that eats only plants

hibernate go into a deep sleep for winter

humid damp air, containing a lot of water

insectivore animal that only eats insects

mite small parasite that lives on another animal and sucks its blood

omnivore animal that eats meat and plants

parasite tiny animal that lives in or on another animal and feeds off it

particle tiny piece of a substance

pollution making the environment dirty with waste or poisonous chemicals

predator animal that hunts and eats other animals

prey animals that are hunted and eaten by other animals

reptile cold-blooded, scaly animal, like a lizard or snake

shed lose skin or hair

species type of similar animals that can have babies together

ultraviolet a type of light

venomous having a poisonous bite

vitamin special chemical that animals need to stay alive

vivarium a special tank for keeping lizards in

Index